MAY DARKNESS RESTORE

MAY DARKNESS RESTORE

Poems

Sean Sexton

Press 53
Winston-Salem

Press 53, LLC
PO Box 30314
Winston-Salem, NC 27130

First Edition

Cover Image, *Allegory of Work*, 72" x 84" oil on canvas,
copyright © 1999 by Sean Sexton.
Used by permission of the artist.

Cover design by Kevin Morgan Watson and Christopher Forrest

Author photo by Clyde Scent

Library of Congress Control Number
2018965760

Printed on acid-free paper
ISBN 978-1-941209-96-7

For Sharon

Michael, Julia and Brian,
and our newest, little
Georgia Marie

Acknowledgments

Grateful acknowledgment is given to editors of the journals in which the following poems, occasionally in different versions, first appeared:

Apalachee Review, "Elsewhere"
Cimarron Review, "Day's Work"
Dry Crik Review, "Out of Season Calves," "The Empty Tomb,"
    "You Got Your Pocket Knife on You?" "Early Hour"
Eno, "Mud"
Kestrel, "The Leftover Cow," "Stepping Between the Strands"
MiPOesias, "Moon Hens"
South Florida Poetry Journal, "Things Found Caught in the Fence,"
    "Not," "Last of the Calves," "The Barren Heifer"

This volume features some selections previously published in two chapbook collections: *The Empty Tomb* by the University of Alabama's Slash Pine Press, 2013, and *Descent* by Yellow Jacket Press, 2017.

"A Judgment" was featured in *Ode to Treasure Hammock Ranch*, a film produced by Heather Godwin, *Spiritpaddle Films*, which debuted as an official selection at the 2012 Global Peace Film Festival, Winter Park, FL.

"Old Fence Posts" was presented at the 29th Annual National Cowboy Poetry Gathering during a panel discussion, *Agriculture and the Creative Muse.*

Special thanks as well to Laurel Blossom, Susan Boyd, Rick Campbell, Elizabeth Friedmann, Alice Friman, Linda Hussa, Michael Kemp, Donna Long, Campbell McGrath, Warren Obluck, Gianna Russo, Emma Trelles, Andy Wilkinson, and Claude Wilkinson. I give deep-felt gratitude to Carissa Neff, Steve Bradbury, and Sidney Wade who read and contributed to this volume immeasurably throughout its creation. Lastly, I cannot say enough to characterize the wonderful relationship forged throughout the editing process of this book with Christopher Forrest. His uncompromising generosity and grace for my words and life set a standard only consigned to legends in his trade. I am deeply grateful for his love made visible on these pages, and the faith, imagination, and assurance of Press 53 editor in chief, Kevin Watson. I cannot finish without citing my dear friend, Alfred Corn, who has been kind to me in Poetry in every imaginable way. He is truly one of the sweetest souls and greatest poets of our time.

Contents

A Judgment

Stepping between the Strands

May Darkness Restore

One of the great dreams of man must be to find some place between the extremes of nature and civilization where it is possible to live without regret.
—Barry Lopez

All I've ever wanted to say in my writing is that I love the world.
—E. B. White

The Weeks of Calves

Autumn has a fragrance the cold imparts, perhaps, but today the cold has temporarily left, and that fragrance is even more noticeable. It is the odor of past autumns as well, which makes it remembrance in part, but against the warm, heavy air of many weeks ago, it is something entirely its own. I hear calves out in the dark before morning, a number of them at once as if they're having a calf-party in the pastures to the east. And an occasional reply—a kind of location finding, concerned bleat from a mamma cow, keeping certain bearings between them—as good old, experienced cows constantly do throughout the day. They don't always answer each other. In fact, they aren't above outright torturing one another, the way human children and parents at times refuse to communicate with one another. It flows both ways. You can hear a cow running around the field searching everywhere, crying like a woman who misplaced her purse, while her calf is off in oblivion, playing with his cohorts. Likewise, a calf that can't find his mammy might walk the fence line, bawling for her as she's out there with her head down among friends, grazing to beat the day. As well, and somewhat mysteriously, there are those who set their calf down in the grass where he stays, not another word spoken, until she comes back for him, whether that turns out to be an hour or a week later.

We found the little one out among patches of leftover summer weeds in the back of the pasture after the cows moved. We thought we were safe shutting the gate once they all went through but I said to Young Boss, *Let's go check and make sure we got 'em all.* Sure enough that little thing was out there, all ears on our approach. *I don't ascribe to his mammy's style of managing him,* I said to Young Boss. We didn't have a rope but we got out and tried to get close. He rose in full caution of us, started away, but made a kind of circle back that yet didn't bring him close—by his design. It was almost as if he was fleeing and finding us at the same time, and then we realized he was blind. We moved toward him and he veered off into space and we figured we'd best leave him alone until we were better set to deal with him.

We came back with a rope, drove to the spot and found him again. Young Boss caught him, and we let the tail-gate down so he could sit back there and hold him while I drove back to the cows. We put him just inside the gate, in the common area. There were five or six pairs when we arrived, and he wandered among them in his little blind circles, crying quietly, sometimes in answer to distant lowing of mothers in the field. He tried to nurse one close-by mammy, but she kicked him, nearly knocked him to the ground and then he understood and kept to himself.

The milky film that covered his eyes was the same as another calf we found the week before when we came from the south driving through the cows. We tagged 007's calf in a gate after catching and dragging him there to do the trick. She became irate, so we couldn't just pull him up and tag him—she'd eat us alive! We were close enough to the corner that I dallied around the frame of the truck and we drug him the whole way. We finished with all that and saw something to the east Young Boss took to be a lightning-struck cow.

I'd seen that before, late one summer, and crossed rough ground to make sure it wasn't just a lighter'd snag sticking up, maybe sunlit in a way that made it unfamiliar. But there was a certain contortion to it, made me less sure of what I was seeing every step closer I got. They were all in a swale, laid out beneath a tall pine with the tell-tale golden streak furrowing its bark all the way to the ground—three big old cows, two blacks and a brindle, all struck, with a near-term calf three-quarters birthed out of each. Big calves! But I'll tell you, lightning is a sorry-assed midwife.

Young Boss said he thought he saw a cow's leg sticking up. We drove over. She appeared to have been struck, but on closer inspection, we found something at her hind end we'd never seen before. It killed her coming out, but she did get him out. It was eight-legged, two-headed, and joined at the spine; kind of a bovine spider, with things sticking out in every direction—closer to a wire barb than a calf—but easily a hundred and twenty pounds of mess. Her uterus was prolapsed and distended, and the world was already going to work on her—the flies and worms. Wasn't nothing to do but leave her and keep on.

We wound up in the Watermelon Tract, went in through the back gate hoping to get behind the cows and push them to the other end, and we came upon that little thing—emaciated, keeping to where he'd been set down and only half licked off, not moving a muscle.

Think he'd just stay there until he starved to death? Young Boss asked.

Reckon so.

We gathered him up, and in so doing, found his eyes to be of that same milky glass. He was blind, looked in a way like a sightless old Chinese sage, a purely meditative soul whose purpose in this world was to ponder the nature of things—and he weren't doing nothing but that when we found him. We left him in the common area to see who'd claim him while we caught and marked up a few calves, but none would. We took him in, seeing as the only other thing to do was knock him in the head, but we weren't about to do that—not to that little thing. I called a feller who'd stopped by the previous week wanting to buy a brahma heifer for his daughter to show. We'd told him we were low on brahma heifers presently and not selling any, but we'd call him if we ever get a dobie calf, and he seemed thankful we'd consider such a thing.

He wanted the calf, even after we explained it was blind, and came by and got it.

We weren't out of the week when we discovered another mess out among the first- and second-calf heifers. We felt we'd had our share of God's little dark angels this calving season, but there he was, settin' and blinking at us, one front leg short a third of its length, the other an extra third long and turned completely around, twisted so what was up should have been down. His back legs were fused and askew. He was put-together chaos, an unworkable proposition any way you tried to figure him. He'd never stand and nurse, he'd never stand at all, but there he was looking at us as though the day would be fine for us all. She was still licking him off right then, so we decided to let it go a day. It was all just a bit much.

Young Boss said, *He's just coyote bait, he's not going to make it.*

Yeah, I said, *but I ain't ready to do nothin' yet—his mammy's taking care of him for now.*

We prayed he'd be dead when we got out there the next day, but he wasn't.

We took a gun.

She'd gone off to graze or water. He was still in the little depression in the ground where he'd been born.

Young Boss shot him.

It had to be done, but it was like crushing an orchid underfoot. We couldn't just leave him and weren't no way we were bringing that thing home.

It's hard to reckon, but death came to him like a kind of knowledge. You could see it. You could see in his face he knew what kind of world this is.

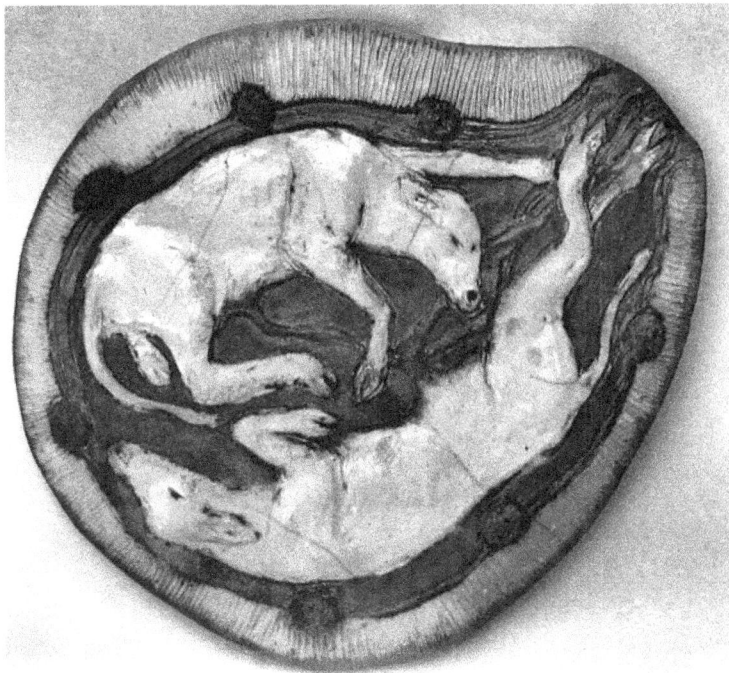

ENVIRONMENTAL AUDIT

Environmental Audit

Last of all she asked:
What are the bare places
in the aerial. . . all over this block—
Did you bury toxic waste out there?

I examined the map a moment.
No. It's a male thing—this is our bull pasture.
This is where they spend nine months apart from the cows
every year, digging holes and bellerin'.

The Prosperous Year

Today with the cattle grows the cash,
consigning debt to an easier portion,
resting minds, filling pockets, greening grass,
like morning rain fresh off the ocean.

A warm, wet winter kept the bulls active,
and shortly, Spring took over the land.
A tired old world made on sixty-cent calves
has resurrected into something grand.

Prosperity ruins us to a man—
lucre for the prudent and mistaken.
All's I can say is get it while you can,
and pray once asleep, hardship won't waken.

As mammon joins our most common vices,
the cure for high prices—is high prices.

The Jubilant Calf

The just-born jubilant calf,
no sooner on his feet
and he's bucking, cavorting,
exalting, in this world.

He's wet as if he'd just waded from a ditch
his shabby feet soft to the sharp, dry thatch.
Yet how he plies them
in his wobbly dance,

kicking the sky
with no idea of his station
in the morning light.
In an hour he could outrun a lion,

and breathlessly hide in a clump of grass.
For now he celebrates
his own great accident—
newling of life's happenstance.

How Vultures Eat a Cow

The first work is invisible, tongue
swiped from its shelf in tasty pecks,
the skyward eye plucked from its hollow,
the earthbound soon to follow,
nostrils mined, seized lips,
and soon the party spills aft—
for lunches of softness, genitalia, teats,
self-served in bites and nips.

The interior gains in a thousand tears,
despoiling halls, tapestries of flesh.
The extravagances of being ruined grandly;
fixtures, furnishings, décor stolen slowly.
O, the fabrics, finery, and accouterments
stripped to mere architecture. A weeklong
gnaw into darkness and the hardening,
souring breath of the air, as microbes

prepare sauce on the world's behalf—
digestion's benevolence in aftermath.
Through leering windows in dapples and stripes,
the empty frame casts the rise
and set of the orb on girdling tide
of russet grass, and pummeled earth.
Not a year or two will take what's left,
not bones, teeth, or even thought.

Moon Hens

She put down and opened a white plastic crate, released
five pale, disheveled hens from the research farm,
where they'd hung in cages like moons in a twilight barn,
high above the ground.

Their stations were devised to hold water and grain,
catch their pallid eggs and drain away excrement.
They've come to earth like astronauts
from months in space, barely able to stand.

The ground for them is an unfamiliar puzzle, variety sudden,
brightness a foil. They'll find themselves if they can,
peck by peck, in the minutia of grains and moving things.
May the dewy grass summon their wakening

into a dailiness of what to find, what to leave, written
in a world that will prune the long crescents
of their unshorn claws, each a waned
sliver about to set and be hidden in light.

Lowly Estate

The floor of the pens has drowned
in its burden of sky
and become a tree-faced mirror
for a season, limned
in posts, boards, leaves and vines,
set into shadowy shine.

During gatherings as the cattle arrive,
a mute voice rises
from a thousand hoof beats,
and the mud gobbles fear's impress
as they sink in its throat
to their knees.

At the end of the work,
the herd flies through the gate
like water down an opened sluice
toward the fawning green
and evening breeze, deserting
what must stay.

The mud shuts quietly,
solace in its face,
swallowing, stiffening, drying
at the pace of a failing oak,
unattended, wordless,
until it breaks.

Loss

For Claude Wilkinson

It is sad
to speak a poem
of vanished things:

spreading adder, dung beetle, meadowlark—
all gone
to a faraway morning.

Golden orb weavers
absent from heaven's windows
and spring evening

fireflies
lasting to early fall—exiled
into gloom.

Fox squirrel,
box turtle, glass snake,
fragrances, accesses, whole vistas,

even starlight—mortal as dew,
their disappearance by
convenience and dearth our due diligence.

Recompense comes
with summers eternal, gain in skies full of birds,
all of them black.

The Unseasonable Year

With a First Line by William Logan

Becalmed in the loose days, calmer in storm,
though winter failed to claim the fields.
Our cultivars perished weeks shy of the warm,
following drought's diminishing yield.

April's first morning we took out the bulls
in lack of forage, risings of thistles;
thereafter spring, decadent, vertical,
flourished with pigweed and soda apple.

Noon's daily, cauterizing hour,
ruined any chance of gain,
fixing our plight and waning power
over a rift grown between hope and disdain.

To seasons beyond we ply our ways,
and pray a wind for better days.

Physiology of Bovine Reproduction

For Campbell McGrath

Actions of acids afford amniotic adherence to adjunct appendages
building a body of blastocysts, broached between bladder and brisket,
causing chromosomic communication, capacitation, and contractions,
determining derivations of deoxyribonucleic descendance,
ensconcing estrogen-enhanced eggs, evoking erection, ejaculation,
and embryos,
following factors in fallopian tubes, featuring follicle, fertilization,
and finally, fetus,
grown of gravid gametes, germ plasm, and glands,
helping hormone held horns, hypothalamic and hot with
infundibular involvement, inflamed and implanted,
joining jurisdictional juices, juxtaposing
kinesis and kinship,
leveraging labial loosening, labyrinthine ligaments, and luteal liberation,
matters moreover of mammary, milk, and in misbegotten moments,
mastitis.
Next to nucleic acids, nothing is new—
owing oogenesis, ovulation, and occurrences of the oviduct,
proffering puberty, penetration, pregnancy, and parturition,
qualifying each year's produce, quantifying
rampant reproductive responses,
solving for sex, season, and semen quality—
trials for testes and tract,
uterus, and ultimately udder,
vesicles, and vulva, verifying
what does or does not happen between the
X chromosome and the
Y, yet all within the
zona pellucida, a zygote is fashioning.

Calving Season in the Tropics

As autumn days upend our senses,
the tropics wield their reckonings,
and heaven's breath brings summer's end
and harm of winter's beckoning.

They come like rain of hidden storms—
produce shook from starry thresh
as gravid clouds—expectant forms
bring torrents of determined flesh.

Through onslaught and lull, unrelenting,
no forecast given, no lame foretelling;
beyond disappearance and fateful finding
to reconcile nine months' swelling.

Arriving into the world's firm grasp,
The last shall be first, and first shall be last.

Things Found Caught in the Fence

A late April Inventory

Innumerable wisps of cow's tails:
silken, black, tawny, and brown.
Tiny spider webs
(tent-fashioned & occasional)
on wire barbs.
A single white tuft of down.

Remains of the butcher bird's quarry:
2 frogs (desiccated), a locust,
baby red rat snake, draped,
3 small beetles, dark, shiny,
impaled—
and hollowed out.

Dew.
A buckthorn bush, privet,
and several thistles
grown up and through.
Four equal-sized, ongoing spaces.
Light.

Resurrection Fern

In firewood piled
two seasons deep,
tendrils emerge
like Christ,
transcending death
upon a tree,

a felling and
breaking,
the crush of the tomb.
They peer out like Lazarus
from their gnarly vantage
into the fire.

Any gain
in this realm,
is always
something's ruin.
Every life—
a resurrection.

Landings

If I don't see you in the future, I'll see you in the pasture. . .
—Anon.

The world visits the pasture on occasion with escaped brightly-colored heliums importing messages of birthday or anniversary, dragging a shred of party ribbon like a tattered umbilical from the navel of a week-old calf. They arrive infrequently at fair time, collapsed, exhausted zeppelins, landed in smut grass clumps or snagged on fences. Once, a middle schooler's science-project balloon appeared with a self-addressed card to return like a felled mallard's leg band, documenting parameters of direction, duration, and distance, and the rule nothing flies forever.

A weather balloon crashed in the far field with a cargo of damaged instruments and we found honeycombed, titanium fragments of an airplane's hull scattered in the block where we keep the little bulls. We deemed them inessential, or we'd have the whole bird on our hands, as when a crop-duster, attempting a *touch-and-go* in the lane to the cow pens, *touched,* but *go* didn't work, and he walked out, unexcused and unseen. To this ground comes the manifold tears of heaven, fallout from masses of warm and cool air bringing mist and deluge, lightning and ice.

A sudden incursion of ashes out of the sky from burning too far away to detect, and hidden transports of thistle down or fennel seed suddenly fill whole tracts with their spawn from mysterious remove—so we say: *This is a thistle year*, or ask, *How is it we suddenly have dog fennel everywhere?* We rarely understand our sudden misfortune, yet in nature, multiplication is prodigious and certain, sourcing stands of soda apple, Brazilian pepper, briars, and pigweed from scat in the tracks of vermin, droppings of birds and the embrace of the wind.

And each autumn, in advancing darkness, the cattle begin, one by one, to wander and search lonely places to disgorge their late summer's burden: calves, hundreds, as though here is where life deigns to appear, come to earth and be found among the flotsam and jetsam of the universe.

Coyote's Work

All that remains is
the tiny skull,
spine,
pelvis,
and ribs,
cartoon of life,

or mannequin of death.
A core of something
sparsely rendered—
hide, extremities,
scattered,
missing.

Pieced together,
aside of loss:
See the addled young cow,
her listless birthling
no sooner born
than taken.

Grant them hunger's
importunity,
the *yip-yip-yelping*
and hysterical creature delight
sounding the dark, settling again
the pressing weight of their lives.

Weaning Song

For Enid Shomer

At week's end, seven sun-filled
mornings since that day's passing,
hot, bright, clear, windless as an eye,
when killing anything would be easy,
I heard their voices ringing blue
from dark to day's full light.

And the next morning's light,
in empty cow pens fully
trodden, softly an early wind blew
as if from the past.
The task had finished easily
as snuffing a candle or shutting an eye.

By the second evening, I
took the cows home in waning light.
Hungry and quiet they went, easing
along to pasture, paths filled
with them passing
as the sinking orb made crimson of blue.

Calves stand in the open blue
with bleating cries and wakened eyes
through five mornings passed
in another world's light.
The fence lines trodden, corners full,
they crowd for warmth lost so easily.

Remembrance comes to them easy
these still mornings breaking to blue
over pastures strange, they fill,
beneath a constant, burning eye
grazing, growing in the light,
until a month has passed.

A season rolls past.
The year turns quickly, easily,
away from the light,
less day than night, more fire than blue.
From darkened skies and quiet eyes,
tomorrow's fields will fill

as empty heaven to fullness of light.
So easily they've come and gone.
I hear them passing into the blue.

Planting Aeschynomene Seed

It pours from a muslin sack like sunlight
through a cracked window shade, fifty pounds
to a metal washtub, old as your footsteps.
A musk, carnal to the world, rises from
the emptying breath of particles almost
too tiny to see, or believe.

Three handfuls of buttermilk splashed from a cupped palm
upon the grains and my father is there, again showing how
as I've watched half my life on planting days. His arms like ladles
work wetness through, scraping bottom in steep swipes as if
he was cleaning the tub with seed, raising slurries to mix
in the isolate drys, and work done well—a pearly sheen
coats every hull.

My pocketknife in a dull crackle cuts the packet of inoculant.
Rhizobium leguminosarum, suspended in black, moldery peat
is poured in grabs, shook out on the surface. Churning hands
return, mixing the dark warmth as if stirring a shadow
into the seed, until a spot
touches every speck.

Math he scrawled on a torn scrap of sack—readily as his name
on Friday's paycheck—I've kept my whole life: the quartered-
mile in feet times the spread, measured with a stretched cloth tape
behind the tractor. Blades are spinning, seed wasting. The down
and back is divided by 43,560—denominator of our lives,
for the fraction of an acre covered every round.

We use an elderly scale, softly sprung, the numbers barely legible
to mete out the pounds of seed, and, remainder weighed on return,
adjust the gate. Five acres you hoist and dump into the hopper,
twenty more stacked in bags on the tailgate, to treat as the tractor
takes flight, flinging microbes as it goes—and it all seems possible,
given of history, procedure, machinery, ingredients, and a small
measure of hope.

Nest Eggs

Yesterday morning I prepared the roe of the mackerel queen
my son caught on a Saturday morning off-shore excursion.
I exhumed two swollen, pink, vein-bound bags from the silver
damsel, and sliced them into pieces to sauté.
I lament her demise, eggs never laid, fish lives
that never will be—eaten and relished with shame.

And the pea-hen that set five eggs in our dooryard
at the foot of St. Francis beneath the penumbra of a sapling
as we watched in awe of her poorly chosen nest, her
unfaltering devotion to the task. She'd stand
a moment, shift the eggs like a careful cook frying
chicken pieces, managing warmth, and some kind of order.

The curvature and needling devise of her beak revealed
its perfection for such, as did her shape, crouched
like morning fog upon a hollow. Day or night, rain or shine,
she stayed. In a downpour at dusk, we tried to help her,
swiped a shower curtain from the guest bath, to drape
in the branches of the tree, affixed with clothespins
and best of intention. We left a radio blaring through the night,

wakened to crying, same as last month's hen that hatched
three fuzzy balls with legs she led half a week, feeding,
gathering them in when they strayed, until in a single
obliterating moment they were taken. For days she wandered
yelping, searching aimlessly. Now shells lie asunder
like smashed crockery. She's afoot and again, loose in the air—
that sound the world makes.

DISPARATE

———————

Query

Will this one day end—
working on a ranch,
living close to nature—

your fullness astride me
in retreating darkness
silky skin rising

and falling
through my hands
like soft light.

There is lowing
outside in the distance,
not a leaf stirs.

Each day
is my last
in paradise.

Boy or Girl

"It don't matter which you get—"
Herman Thomas said, closing the gate
of his loaded truck to market;
the morning of the day
of our daughter's birth.
"If it's a girl, you can make her into a man!"

On the Peter Pan Bus Between Boston and New York

Love and happiness make for strange
accommodations, yet amazing to me
this morning is the attractive,

dark-haired young woman
just passed up the aisle,
now crouched and pissing

behind the plastic and steel
folding door—
three feet away—

as we roar through
the early spring barrens of
New England.

Elko

At the National Cowboy Poetry Gathering

Mona's Divas—*open noon to four a.m.*,
Sue's Fantasy Club, Number One
Geisha, and Inez's *Dancin' and Diddlin'*,
thrive on streets behind the Stockman's Casino,
where I'll have 6 a.m. coffee with Vess Quinlan
at the counter and watch the day grow old.

———

The Rubies glitter just past this hour, in a pristine sky
over buildings and parking lots half-filled with cars, SUVs,
trucks and stock trailers, that struggled through, dressed
in mud and fresh fallen snow. The ground is tricky
and hard as rock in a frozen stream. Days and hot grease
run together in places that don't shut down for those who
won't leave.

———

It's almost time for coffee with Vess,
words under his arm and history in every footstep.
I pass the Jet Coin Laundry with its windows of whirling
clothes—somebody always washing something.
Reams of cardboard stacked and bound, accrete solemnly
against the Pioneer Hotel, in the lot beside the grocery.

———

Last night a soul made yellow snow
in a small draw between buildings, set down his
drink to do so. Street receptacles overflow
with glasses still full of ice, straws
and butts, of purposes lost as posters
in early light-shine of the hotel windows.

———

Vess and coffee await, "*Sheep raised dust*" in his thoughts,
lanolin rubbed posts in a place as far as memory
can lay hold. I step off the curb as vehicles
slow, stop as I cross, wait like the horse at Capriola's,
to go somewhere. The leftovers at "Goldies" dance
behind smoked glass, in their antechamber of night.

———

Half-said in half-extinguished bulbs,
Liberal Slots is spelled in the marquis
of the Commercial Casino, and beckon the insane
with *Girls! Girls! Girls!* as high above, a grand,
erect polar bear whose appellation *White King*
could make sense here, if not just anywhere.

———

The ancient, gray stone Post Office
is centered upon the square,
where I step around a huge, dull, platter of ice—
"*Mirror seen through dimly, but then face to face,*"
that never liquefied nor shrank during my sojourn
in Elko. Vess—keep my place. I'll be along soon.

Meditation Upon Dutch Boy General Purpose Paste Flux

See the plastic screw-capped container of Dutch Boy
General Purpose Paste Flux, left by the man summoned
to tear out a wall of our bathroom closet, replace
and solder pipes buried deep inside,
now exposed after twenty-five years.

Though he is old, the Dutch Boy's face is younger than
the face of our youngest child, gone from this house;
his room down the hall, empty but for a few childhood
effects, bed once unkempt, now tidy and made,
only slept in by infrequent guests.

And I've never heard of the Dutch Boy or his paste flux,
though he spans more than twice my years, and I realize,
as on my first trip to Chicago, how little known
this world has been to me, how long mankind
has carried on in conventions of artifice

and pleasure, industry and depravity, whose remainders
stand in unsolvable riddles of time. Only these
and occasioned stories bear a former age, offer
the battered, enduring face of a world
that will still be here when we're gone.

Sunrise, Moonset at 30,000 Ft.

For Linda Hussa

The envelope of air
that contains us, turns
upon a blue, soft sphere
evidenced by rising sun,

setting moon and clouds
above a hidden floor,
like fleeces, scattered
as though a shearer

had labored
through the night
and left the gather
for morning light.

Disparate

The girls in the museum cafeteria titter in
pleasant gossip, coiffed and garbed alike
in gold, cashmere, and silk. Each face keeps
the same joy in this holiday escape from dailiness.
as their secret society, founded upon commiseration,
excludes a Venus in synthetic leopard wrap the next
table over, her long, raven hair mussed as if
she'd just stepped from a baroque bedchamber.
She has nothing to say to them (nor do they ask),
but sits attending an old, blind Tobit and his
wife sipping water and taking a frugal repast.

Morandi's lonely bottles hang in the galleries upstairs,
paintings in lush pink butter and almond paste,
and the most exquisite greys in art. On a wall placard
is a quote from his ending days:
*"If only you knew Longhi, how badly I want to work,
I have so many ideas I wish to develop. . . "*
In quiet and solitude he kept at his métier, sharing
the family apartment with his three unmarried sisters,
seeking only the recognition of his peers—the leering Chardin,
rag tied round his bespectacled head, stolid Piero, mercurial
Caravaggio, and the intractable, enraptured, Cézanne.

The Last Hard Parts

Someday your last hard parts will be
discovered scratched off a road,
dug out of a ditch, held
in rock or scattered by the sea:

bits of tooth, knuckle, and nail,
or fragments of a shell
outlasting water and wind,
fire and cold.

Traces of old meanness arisen
from enshrouding bracken
like quartz from clay,
where you last lay

and settled among the dust
of your little certainties,
remains of intransigence,
further standing the test

of time, evidence
you wish couldn't
be found, of the emptiness
in a human heart.

Above Portland

Each moment redraws the mountain
above the city from the Rose Test Garden,
on these seldom clear hours of evening,
Mt. Hood, omniscient, glimmering.

A century ago, Hassam painted here,
where blossoms swallow dusking air,
as stars awaken overhead
in heaven's darkling flower bed,

delighting tourists at the end of day,
who acquiesce to stop and stay
and watch the mountain meld in glare
and ever slowly disappear.

I Thought

I thought the floor was wet
when I stepped on a penny,

and called myself plain-spoken
til I heard plainer speech.

I believed I could see,
until light revealed
I'd memorized the dark.

Sketches of Georgia, 70 MPH

From a mid-winter bull buying trip to South Carolina just before breeding season

The sky at twilight,
well past the border,
is pink as a pink bedsheet.

–

There's a change in feeling at the state line,
difference in the body politic, or perhaps
history's grain running a different direction.

–

A road-side haze, soft, tangled,
perched upon space—
pecan orchard.

–

After seventy-five miles, we find
the fruit and pecan stand
is all sign.

–

Tiny birds over ploughed ground
thousands at dusk, swarming
like birdshot, from a fired gun.

–

Towns fly by—Adel, Cordele, Hahira, Macon:
mythical places where the old black men of my upbringing,
now dead and gone, were from.

–

"The newness is wearing off," my father says
as darkness begins to set—and will be gone
before we're out of Georgia.

Over the West in Flight

Inbound to "Lost Wages, NV"

Nothing below is the color of my life:

Absence of water stories the land in lies—
misplaced ocean, ancient stream courses
etch a past, auspicious.

Wind fields sparsely populate vantages
with white propellers on posts
turning lazily synchronous.

Sheep clouds graze in flocks
of shadows on the mountaintops,
above circles of failing crops—

beige, grulla, russet, and blonde
as where scalding pots were set down
the last ten miles to town.

From a Café Window—8 AM, Washington, DC

Pedestrians hasten by outside.
An Amerasian woman rounds the corner
in her SAAB, driving her brief
automotive history around town.
There's something in her face,
stark as a written page
the day will turn.

The line to the counter beside my table
is a human highway, it's movement halting,
indeterminate. At the head, a black woman
tends her register. She's blunt, down to business,
caught in a universe of transaction, has things
her way, giving commands to the air,
such that I missed mine, had to be told
twice, but was forgiven, my money taken.

In this hour, the windows fill with faces
flowing past in confluences of flesh
as the sun crawls out of bed
above the thickening traffic
where life seems a long,
protracted wait
for the certainty
of its end.

11:30 PM [After Listening to Brahms's 1st Piano Concerto at the Neighbor's]

At the edge of tomorrow, I share the couch on the terrace
beneath the porch light with our old smelly dog, Annie,
curled, breathing heavily in a kind of peace.
She rolls on her back when I pat her, legs upright.
Cats on the ledge above, crunch feed from a metal pan,
eating contentedly before disappearing into the night.

My cigar burns down.
I'll go to bed when it's gone,
wick of human fire soon to extinguish, and I realize
comfort governs all things of the world: We eat,
drink, breathe in with pleasure its impurities
and then, temporally or eternally, between settings
and risings of the orb, we rest.

A JUDGMENT

Sunday Evening Lament

While we were at church this morning, our neighbor
gathered his herd and hauled calves to the stockyard
for tomorrow's market. His cows are crying tonight,

the sound—so forlorn in the twilight.
In less than a month, another such dirge will rise of our making,
and once again in a season of heartache,

bring to the air a fulsome mourning
for the summer breeze to spread upon the land
and bathe in its blood reckoning.

Out-of-Season Calves

appear one day, revealing
things gone wrong
in the irretrievable
past.

How they flesh out neglect,
holes in fences, unperceived short-
comings in one's plans.
Yet there they are—

robust, sprightly creatures
shimmering in the morning light
like new leaves.
Dear to whom they've come

as breath itself, misbegotten
signs of what, pray,
shall ever keep in
this world.

Early Hour

In this hour the light
barely holds the sky
and enters our room.
Enough for love's secret toil
and aftermath, things small
as this light, overwhelmed
by the world it wakens.
See the moon's nimble

crescent
gleaming above the palm trees,
a frog on every trunk climbing
through saffron glow to bed.
A single bird voices
the last dim clarity
before rising mists
untenure our dreams.

A Judgment

The gate slides open,
and a heifer steps on the scales.
You consider whether to keep her
as she stands trembling, weighs 540,
and the cut-off is six.
And the question: *What do you think?*
is in the air, traveling man to man
through the crew, is in your mind
as you peer between the boards—
weighing this, weighing that. . .

The trailer to market is backed against
the loading chute.
Open one gate, and she returns to pasture,
to what she's always known;
the other, a portal to the world,
uncertain place for lives cut loose.

Is she too refined—
not enough bone and frame,
muscling that doesn't carry through,
an imagining that fails
in flesh?

She'll make a cow—
might otherwise be thought,
spoken aloud in resolve,
or *Sell her!* proclaimed
if only softly to one's self.

By an utterance—gates shift
and swing, and life,
whichever way,
swallows a cow
whole.

The Barren Heifer

Today is the day, the last crimson dawn
for the barren heifer, a truck to the abattoir,
soon to arrive. Half a year she stayed,
up to her withers in feast in the set-aside
pasture, with orphans, errant bulls,
a rickety cow, and others on last legs.

We drove her with an ancient, blind dam
who knew the gate, stored them together
overnight in the pens to keep her blood quiet.
She has no light, no soil within to plant.
Dinner by dinner, we'll send her to heaven,
our bellies her path, one way or another.

Mud

There's a story of the cocksure dairyman
who formed and poured his parlor, stoop,
and alleys with concrete, swearing then,
"I'm finished with mud for good!"

Three days, four rains, nine milkings logged
and where the cows come, gather and wait—
near the landing, out beyond the gate
stands a small, intractable bog.

Digging out the squeeze chute
for tomorrow's workday, I face
a mass, hoof-pocked and raised,
mud from a month ago or more,
keeping the catch, holding the door
in its frozen embrace.

Time's foundation and hull—
I chop, topple and scrape,
prying hidden seams apart,
breaking in chunks by shovelsful,
working emptiness up the chute,
blade by jamming blade.

This was what cattle slogged through,
heft and overburden of the land
carried to this cell of reproof,
grabbing them leg by ambling leg,
to mold and cast their haste
as we gained the upper hand.

Swallowing rain and spewing dust,
endured like bad government,
unbidden guests, the mud belongs to us.
Joining high ground, borrowing low,
never wanted, or where supposed,
the mud belongs to us.

The Empty Tomb

For Casey Baggott
Why do you seek the living among the dead?
—Luke 24:5

What might have been a fallen star,
glittering in the distance
became the dreaded sight—
a heifer in trouble, calving.

But she was dead, still warm,
her uterus prolapsed:
half its length inside out, entwined
in torn placenta;

a useless vision shaped of
heartache and awe,
to abandon with all thought
of her.

But the calf
must still be inside.
How was he lodged?
What went wrong?

I tried to push in and find him.
Tides of flesh kept me out.
I cut across the tissues with my knife,
opened her, loosing a wash of blood.

I removed and set
aside the mass,
reached in
to emptiness.

He must be out, I thought—
as I walked in circles around her,
searching clumps of grass for him—
but nothing.

I left,
drove toward cows in the distance,
noticed in the woods
a small, dark form,

soggy and disheveled,
nursing the knob of a tree,
roots, weeds, sucking any—
and everything.

I caught, bound, and carried him home
and called on the phone
for someone to take him:
Do you want a baby red-brahma bull?

Cousin Rob said he'd sworn off bottle-raising calves,
but a brahma bull—too much to resist.
Save him for me, he said,
I'll be by.

In the pen, he sucked boards and posts, climbed
through the shed, sucking things stored there;
sucked my hands, pants, the gate
as I tricked him to escape.

Colostrum, I thought,
is out there in her.
He won't be worth a shit without it,
old timers would say.

I couldn't go out there again, but—I couldn't not go.
So I found the blue bucket on a shelf,
rinsed a cup and empty milk jug, and
ten minutes later—

udder by udder,
half-blind in the full light of day,
I'm stripping out
a dead cow.

It comes cold with every grasp, hissing into the cup.
Fingers tired, I stop—add it to the jug,
continue, hands sticky, aching, keeping on
until there's no more.

Warmed on the stove, poured into the bucket,
and moments later, I'm coaxing a nipple into his mouth,
little teeth cutting me as I hold his muzzle and squeeze
his jaw open and shut till the rhythm catches.

Soon he's enlivened, autonomous,
tail wagging, tongue working,
swallowing the elixir
of life.

Not

After Seamus Heaney

Not the listless woods these days,
their ongoing summer song
same as the year-round sound in my head.

Not the thick, bottomless mud in gateways
hard as winter to cross, or
the next unbridling rain,

wrung from any torporous hour—
dark, light, morning, night,
nor the suffocating breath

in the sun-soaked air, but you,
four years gone come September,
like a whole calf crop one quick day,
with only us to say you were here at all.

Old Fence Posts

Cut before days were kept, this remainder—
glittering, lichened, stacked between two trees,
bellies, arms, legs, of a long ago gather,
hewn to lengths, shorn of ankles, feet, and knees.
Now missing where they soughed and stood,
from rooted arisings of what was good.

Hauled in plenty from fresh-pushed stands
along a strand, thrown from a mule wagon,
each five paces, post to hand—
post to hand. Set and plumbed, one by one,
against emptiness; the light of cathedrals
vanished with missing ceilings of needles.

Hymn sings of the wind, now gone quiet
as the men who work in church, collect
the tithe, carry the Eucharist.
Almost supine in curious bents
and stapled along their lengths in places
gauged to the lay upon their faces,

strands to hold the herds and their get.
For duty askance of life and grain,
once keeping a world within and without,
now pulled and piled to be cut and piled again.
Measured, marked, sawn, stood, and split
for fireboxes they are seen to fit.

Quartered with brethren of equal name
resting the andirons in trios and quartets
to breathe into draughts of smoke and flame,
in hissing flurries of sparks and light
escaping as though up a flight of stairs,
to join the quiet, befriending air.

The Beekeeper

He came on Summer afternoons, Tuesdays
at two, punctual as the morning star,
to sit for a portrait, six months after Minnie died.
I suggested this thinking of the good
it would do us both.

He and Minnie kept bees on the ditch banks of the ranch.
I met them going to their yards on my way to lunch,
stopping—truck window to tractor seat, in short conversations
I never quite heard for the noise and his soft-spoken voice
(Minnie watched and nodded, agreeing with things we said).

They'd check the hives midday, when sunlight
and pine-needle smoke would quiet the bees,
treat for wax moth, foul brood, and carpenter ants,
worm and sugar the bees in the stretches between
pepper bloom and orange-blossoms.

How happy they seemed and bereft he became
when she died—news he gave one day when I asked
of her, passing him again along the ditch.
It was like coaxing a wild creature from its hiding place,
getting him into a pose.

He brought his smoker, a frame of foundation,
and jar of honey at my request; wore his green denims
and gray felt hat—I never saw him different in twenty-five years—
sat at the end of the table beside a bouquet
of flowers, folded his hands together, and stared.

I sketched him on a panel in vine coal.
He spoke as he posed, answering my questions
but was mostly silent. We talked about bees,
their odd behavior—the circle dance, royal jelly,
and rituals of handling them:

Move them three ft. or three miles, he said.
We discussed nectar conditions and the nauseous peaks
of spring, when the little cups of bloom are full,
and the odor takes over the land. *Rank—*
Eddie Dancy calls it, I told him, and he nodded.

Born in Oklahoma,
he came here from the engine room
of a destroyer in the South Pacific, where
he spent the entire war—noise, heat, and
bewilderment of combat, in that kitchen of hell—

where upon any blasting moment, the whole house
could go hurtling to the bottom of the world.
He could but turn his wrenches and keep
himself there—as he kept in his chair,
kept

to the steel Quonset hut of the grove shop,
where he found work, sweltering summers,
and deafening sound, maintaining a cavalry of raggedy-
assed tractors, sprayers, mowers, and equipment rolling through
a universe of frozen bolts and grease.

The painting advanced a little each day
and he'd ask to see it on his way out—gazing upon
his envisagement as one might across an open tract of land.
Yet he'd arrive the next week at the appointed hour
to sit again.

We crept through the season, one day a week, Thursday at times
switched with Tuesday for doctor's appointments, and the ceiling
fans patted our shoulders as our water glasses stood their rings
on the table. I replaced six bouquets in the course of work,
returning props to their pale chalk outlines each time we resumed.

A passing storm that took out the lights, and I, running to shut windows, were the only halts in our progress. Of the vacuous air in which memory flows, drawing event and happenstance as water down a drain, the painting became, pouring from his presence onto the panel, through pigment, media, spirits, and brush.

One day near the finish, he didn't come.
I thought nothing of it, set up and waiting, figured he forgot,
though he would die before doing something unseemly.
Then with no answer to his phone the following week,
I called his neighbor—

Would you go over and check on Mr. Owens? Something might
be wrong. He hasn't come to sit for me and it's not like him.
They found him in bed where he left the world.
Eddie Dancy settled on a price for the bees and equipment
with his daughter from Oklahoma.

I finished the painting from memory,
changing the flowers once more, imagining
him, hands folded together,
sitting among his things
without a word.

You Got Your Pocketknife on You?

I'm wearing my pants, ain't I?
my grandfather would say.

Never go around without a pocketknife
Joe Yates told us,
or someday someone will beat the shit out of you!

Yesterday morning, I sent the boys out to feed the calves.
They hesitated, drove back, yelling, *Throw us your knife,*
we need it to open the bags! Not a blade between them.

This morning, I put on my pants,
fasten my belt, and reach
into an empty pocket.

Flint of Being

Sometimes impermanence takes a long time
—Gretel Ehrlich

The cow's tooth fragment
I found, glittering in the grass,
on a walk in the field—is keen
to the touch as a risen sun in the eyes.

Held against the sky—its jagged sight line
not unlike the basalt peaks of the West,
gives the beast its
hold on the land.

Hard as flints from the Ocala
lime quarries, heaped
beside crushers they'd
ruin rolling through,

an essential accessory,
almost the measure of life,
yet how many empty mouths
mugged on culling day,

which in as many years, raised
twelve calves for the truck?
What remains is stained
of the land's grassy teas, brined

from her four stomachs
concertedly filling,
dissolving, regurgitating
the daily take—

a ballast chewed and swallowed again,
feeding three in one:
calf at her side, the unborn,
and her daily portion,

week by month by year,
through want and plenty,
time's reap and render
all in the mouth of a cow.

Last of the Calves

At the gate, the last of the calves
balk, turn back as toward
some great wisdom, fleeing
to the fond allure of the past,
their last suckle, perhaps—anywhere,
save through that loathsome door
just opened in the world.

The herd has crossed over, resumed its work
yet twenty truants remain, scattering
perilously as if no promise
lay beyond that brink.
Headlong they go, creatures
possessed, close to heaven
as the days they were born.

Transformation

We hauled six loads of dirt
into the front pen,
raised and leveled
the grade—spoiled
all its poetry,
made a dry lot—
good for work,
nothing else.

The Leftover Cow

we discovered
moving the herd to the next pasture
couldn't rise as we drew near.
We dismounted, got behind
to pull her tail and help her up.
She nearly stood—
failing at last, rolling, dropping
like an airplane without wings.

On a third attempt, she's on her feet,
sixteen years old, all hide and bones,
calf just weaned, bag dangling empty
like a gardener's old glove.
I'll bet she's pregnant, my son says
as she ambles through the gate. Surely,
she's infected with life, as with mortal illness, doing
what she's supposed to until she can do no more.

Cow Landays

The ox is on my tongue.
—Aeschylus

Old cows stand in the quiet and wait,
as young cows linger and cry at the empty pen gate.

.

Wrong-chosen bulls, all sent to slaughter
and then what to do with the twenty years of daughters?

.

She limps away in her final week,
more calves weaned than fields full of heifers,
mouths full of teeth.

STEPPING BETWEEN THE STRANDS

———————

On the Path

The eye is a foot on the path
that scales the tangle of smilax,
grapevine, and wild honeysuckle,
does so unscathed by shards
of the shattered mirror
flung to the foliage
from the bright morning.

On the path the foot is an eye,
blind in its shoe, a little less,
unshod, treading warms and cools
of shadow and light.
Whither shall we go as we walk upon
the paths that issue from being—
the pyramid, atop, where sits the eye?

From the etching *On the Path* by Michael Kemp

For Tommy and Sally Jan

On their wedding day

Your love has come like a summer storm.
Before I saw you, I felt you, looming
in the distances of my heart.
When I beheld you, the air turned cool
and full of sound, electricity laced the sky.

Your love is an afternoon rain, filling me,
overflowing deeps made long ago.
You rise like a wind—hurling limbs
and fronds to the ground, loosing leaves
like tears, ransacking my home.

There are no preparations for love,
no windows to shut or doors to bar.
Since you arrived, time is my friend,
desire my assistant, hope—
my map of the world.

See the land—fresh,
dripping and shining
in aftermath,
now become
our waking dream.

Stepping between the Strands

For Robert Taylor Baggott

The fence catches and rips my shirt.
My pants are tattered and worn, seams
unraveling, mud oozing into my boots.

I am Adam tearing out of his clothes,
the world my seeming accomplice.
I feel a raiment of fresh light, the air's
embrace beckoning like spring water,

thrilling every pore. I enter the raucous
silence through its bright, green door.
I recall the place I first wakened,
four years after I was born—

names of things
pouring through my mind
like wind in the trees
at the edge of the yard.

Descent

She has her father's hands,
small and delicate on him,
and ears of the old man
made in pearly skin.

His features, fair and slight,
best imagined on another,
have crossed a great divide
reaching from his mother.

We walk around our lives
a panoply of parts,
all with the he and she of it
tangled in our hearts.

Dealing with a Fire-Breathing Dragon

For my son

She understands space and gives
you none, arriving at the gate
in brindled fury, calf
at her feet, caught
and pulled up to tag.

She snorts, roars.
She will destroy you,
hold you accountable
for every ill
of the universe.

You somehow reach in,
weather her wrath,
finish the job, loose the rope,
and get away, swearing to yourself
to breed her daughter to a gentle bull.

Fence

The strand we take down is old,
barely lithe enough for coiling
into crumbled hoops for gather.
Yet something of a fence remains,
naked posts askew, a division
all along, for and against, where
trees grew in—keeping, like a story,
what was said in first telling.

We'll run new wire, twist ends
into eyelets to hook to and tie,
raise a shine across the break,
crank taut, nail and wrap—*tension,
the reason of wire*—make certain
our intent signifies
and we see ourselves for what we've done
upon this ground, beneath these skies.

Scraping an Old Palette

On the occasion of painting a self-portrait at sixty

I take down from the wall
and scrape an ancient palette;
twenty-five years of paintings launched
from this encrusted, mildewed slab.
A hillside of white lead, cadmium and titanium
heaped like the banks of a river bed,
molder along its outer edge.

Against this demise,
I ply a chisel in strokes,
breaking through tinted strata,
first scraping, then pounding with
a hammer, lifting dried paint, and bits
of wood, gouged from its substance.

Red, orange, and yellow
evict from their neighborhood reluctantly.
There's a dismal heat and softness inside
despite many years' slumber.

So much else frozen—
greens and umber flint-like, fugitive crimson
Prussian and ultramarine blue: dark, stabile
ponds, brittle as glass.

Oxides turned metal,
siennas and ochres become hardened
drouthy earth, Indian yellow fractures like amber—
and the geology of vision, strips in chunks

with makings of grass, bark, leaves,
sunlit rises, and hammocks of trees,
dark ravines, whole tablesful of subjects
crumble into the can beneath.
Intent unbinds, cascading with each stroke,
as dusty prisms configure above
the disintegrating, damnable failings
of perception. Things warm or cool,
both at times.

Primary,
secondary,
tertiary color
and modern chemistry
descending:
dioxazine
diarylide
anthraquinone
isoindoline
pthalocyanine
quinicidrone—
the Bureau of Standards' meager
replacements for magic and scarcity.

What was once protean and lustrous,
ground in luminous oil,
has become
vitreous rain.

And beyond all manual work—
    machines: wheels, belts, grinding discs,
        clogging with world, abolishing semblance,
            all collusion of thought and hand.

The surface reimburses
in nothingness—as clearing
one's throat to speak—
felling forests, razing temples,
draining streams, and listen:
you can hear the sky
crashing softly to the ground.

For Emma Trelles

Elsewhere

Suddenly, you turn a corner and shining
off a green lawn, beneath vivid sky—
an elsewhere

reflecting from windows or shadowed
within lurid depths through the door
to a place you could live.

Here are trees, hedges, and forms
along the walkway, a neighborhood
that seems familiar,

horizon you'd know
in the dark—
and land in your dreams.

———

Have you wakened each day
in the wrong morning and the
leaves, fruits, and pods in the streets,

fallen year upon year without you
on byways to places
you might have gone?

Is this the fragrance of your life,
its true light in your eyes,
and coolness on your face?

Is this where you should have been
all the while you were
elsewhere?

Vision

Suddenly you arrive at an intersection, lights red, traffic frozen and in an instant recognize disaster, remember its bland face, as that sick feeling climbs inside and you watch again how the world works. A mother duck is rounding the median, crossing with nine tiny hatchlings strung behind. Suddenly, a lean, middle-aged black man is out of his van, afoot, hurrying between cars. The light holds. He's behind them, crouching as he goes, arms spread wide as if to coax and protect the procession, a soul on full display as they cross the desolation of four southbound lanes heading to the far curb. She arrives, mounts first, then the rest, one after the other, hop-climbing as even in final measure of miracle, the man falls back, gathers in the smallest, wayward one—four tries and he's up and over. They flow down the bank into the impoundment and he turns, folds his arms, walks back to his van, smiling like the morning sun.

Early Morning Sunrise

For Danny Frasier, Dean of the Sunrise, with a first line
by William Logan

That awkward hour, the beautiful was loose,
and night's elegy given by morning
with garlands of clouds gilt in the distance
and he—present, coffee-eyed, watching.

Hem upon hem of waters breaking
swaddling mirrors in the trough;
a new-born world bathes in the swelling
tide, never knowing enough is enough.

The first ocean—tall, blue, blown bright,
the second a graft of halcyon days,
all—from the sky's haberdashery of light
to love and behold, thousands of ways.

The week's third rise swung a door in the air—
someone I love gone missing there.

Mother Lode

His words to her were lovely enough to steal,
and thus he was taken before their love had fledged.
She came to Florida, met our father,
began our family. She kept his letters
in two binders we found the summer after
she passed. Now everything revealed
on her ninetieth birthday, missed.

We'd drive to the airport Sundays after breakfast
to see little planes take off and land, she
lingering away from her dank apartment,
craving light like a windowsill plant.
I asked questions of him as we watched.
She shared her worry he'd been a poor pilot,
once landing upside-down, in an apple tree.

He'd entered the Navy to fly, and soon
beautiful letters arrived, missing weekends
with her, summer nights on the Wellsville farm,
starlight seen through the treetops from the damp grass,
warm valences of household dogs, muzzlings of a horse.
One missive affirmed his resolve to carry on
despite a comrade perishing in a crash.

They wed—January 1ˢᵗ, 1948—the invitation:
to the honor of Don and Katherine Herold,
Hunter and Hilly Barrett, 6 PM with friends
and family, in the Pennsylvania farmhouse.
He wore Service Dress Blues, she a comely striped gown,
their vows taken hearthside in the parlor with a roaring fire.
O' what this world can make of surety and loveliness.

She watched the graduation exercise, their departure
in formation from Montauk Airfield, waited on a bench
as time inordinate passed. Three men approached
Mrs. Barrett, there's been an accident.
When they left she rushed to the lavatory, removed
her diaphragm from the night before, hoping
his seed might plant. This was her telling.

The planes came and went and we stayed
until all landed or departed—as though
fortune might turn, and the sky
pay back something owed.

After Wang Wei

For Sidney

No old friends in these mountains
where emptiness begets silence.
What brightens mosses in the deeps
lays eternal blue shadows on the peaks.

MAY DARKNESS RESTORE

Stay

For Laura (Riding) Jackson (in memoriam)

Stay, bright sky, blue as the spiderwort's lease
in excess light among the cousined weeds,
the wheedled growth of well-drained lands
by lanes to the bluff overlooking cerulean—

certainty's equal, pure, large as a name,
the remain of what disappears from touch.
With much still standing—sapling pine, Gumbo-
Limbo, strewn palmetto, periwinkles

wrinkling hems of the late poet's house,
close within drip lines of its eave, coonti
misconstruing its bound like an off-hand
word, rampant in the shadow's ecology,
an etymology, safe, rightly fathomed,
home where the last mind left it to stay.

Day's Work

After he was brought into his room,
we split a cowboy shirt down the back, eased
his bruised arms through the sleeves,
and he assumed the appearance of a sleepy
rancher, taking his noonday nap.

He went to death as to a day's work,
got his shoulder into it as when he was thirteen
working at the dairy, milking a man's worth
of cows before school. He said no to the feeding
tubes in quiet disappointment, having failed

the second swallowing test in the hospital.
Without the news secreted among us he'd been
disabled by a stroke, and any idea of which direction
to head, he closed his eyes, last words already spoken.
A mineral patience entered his face, same as

the afternoon he sat his horse, tied to the caught
heifer—hung-up with a deformed calf I had to puzzle
out of her in the hour and a half it took, and there
he stayed, his pain subsumed as a forest into mist.
Through five days struggle, crossing oceans of breath,

he journeyed between realms, the occult mastery
of heart and human tide at work in slow surcease.
The wait, the pain and distance, all he traversed
to overcome himself as we kept vigil, until
he found the narrow, difficult way out.

Legions

You were hidden from me before this day
and now a decree: *I have lost my father*—
comes to my lips
and legions become visible.

I meet you one by one—
each time, the reddened lids, humidity
rising in your faces, we are
alike, kindred.

I now belong to a fraternity of sorrow,
unwittingly joined.
After today, one of you said,
We are nobody's children.

In Memoriam—Ralph Waldo Sexton 1927–2014

Shirts

A Reprise

And now I come to wear your clothes, shirts
that no longer fit, you barely wore in the end
arranged in piles to divide and sort,
of three sizes—which was the measure of you?

I'll accustom my tastes to them, necessarily
choose their cuts and colors, assimilate snaps,
wishing for buttons, unbegrudge a missing
inch of sleeve and draw your skin upon mine,

assuming your hide, pattern, and hue—
don this sudden wealth overwhelming
my life, this unbidden inheritance
now become shrouds of the everyday.

Three Dried Lemons

In late morning,
the artist is home alone.
Three dried lemons
float upon light
in a shallow pan
set near a window.

25
17
15
staged bath minutes
are lightly etched
in the margin.

From acid to plate
they emerge,
darkening left to right
in a paper mirror
on the eye's wayward shore.

From the etching *Three Dried Lemons* by Michael Kemp

In the Hospital

Your mother's become belligerent, was the hospital's call. The care facility sent her by ambulance after she fell in the dinner hall. Loose from bed, naked, catheterized, unseemly wraith of the universe—ready for the galaxies, dragging her purse of magic golden fluids by its long umbilicus. I put her to bed, tried to explain things with pencil and pad, as she'd lost her hearing device in the turmoil, but she was willful, angry at my answers to her unhappy questions, made another break for the heavens and I pressed her back. She shrieked, *You're hurting me!*—well past reason and forgiveness, and our choice to not tell her of lesions growing in her liver, brain, and breast. I decided to leave, and notified the nurse. None of this is simple, as death so easily puts everything in place.

May Darkness Restore

May darkness restore our youth to these hands.
Life has kept our love in arrears—
time will take us to faraway lands.

Your love has made me a changed man.
You've fed my hunger, allayed my fears.
May darkness restore my youth to your hands.

I feel your skin, your sweet demands.
Open your arms, draw me near;
time will take us to unforseen lands.

As beauty is lost, as troubles expand,
the night will help us find each other
and darkness restore youth to our hands—

I know your secrets, I know your plans.
Beyond our dreams, beyond these years,
time will take us to faraway lands.

To hold you now and understand—
to grasp your feet, to smell your hair,
may darkness restore our youth to these hands,
and light our way through terrible lands.

To Love a Woman

I've held you, know the feel of your shoulders,
cant of your hips, coverings
dressing your bones, how they fit the hand—
hard angles done over long ago in flesh,

with something that amounts to understanding.
These I've known, watching you become,
felt what was taut, hard as desire,
turn pliant and agreeable.

I've learned the art of you;
we are the landscapes of one
another, found, explored, settled
and improved by unwitting standard.

Your breasts rise like the central ridge
of Florida, ancient milk beds, yet comely,
and how you stand after a shower,
a delectation of berries and cream—

fluorescent, dripping, still modest to me.
Your belly, and remaining adolescence,
half a hemisphere of wilderness I've
explored like a child; recesses, caves

replacing so many worlds I might have known
had I not known yours.
We've rendered each other thus: into different
creatures than we'd have become apart.

The array of blessings beneath your arms
when you raise them like a prodded crayfish,
your carriage and comportment
have suited me my whole life.

You run a temperature I didn't know
of human beings, a regular heater
beneath the sheets, and softness to the touch
of your skin, my hands expect.

How can this be reconciled in the grand court
of being, and to which magistrate shall we answer
for our preferences, our unforgiveable lust?
Those ridiculous, big eyes, high-lit when closed,

asleep at noon on the daybed, like a poorly painted,
second-rate, grief-stricken, Renaissance Madonna,
and you could hire them out to mourn
twice daily should you find a market

for your tears.
But other eyes no longer suit me,
eyes I couldn't marry,
forever changed by yours.

There's a wildness, an excessive desire borne
of some native joy in you, to make, decorate, and thus,
glorify our household—a true and continual
reinventing of our existence, with color and life.

You're a *slash and burn* gardener, whose projects
outgrow all human capability. The evidence
crowds our spaces, enlivens us, yet I've
carried the burden of your effects in potfuls,

hauled in on freeze-warning nights,
hurried things from the porch to the rain,
borne the slain orchids, desiccated violets, remains of the
flower arrangements, and your world class remorse—

one of your finest attributes! O' the dirt, dust, cat hair,
dog shit, and fleas of your decisions to bring creatures
into our lives, an enthusiasm insistent upon
life's abundance.

Your snore guides my ship
of sleep into port each night—
how empty and long the dark
when you're gone.

The lifelong search for things
I unknowingly embarked upon, the day we met,
toothpaste caps, spaghetti sauce lids, and the like
fly off and hide in plain sight from you in other realms

only I have infrequent access to.
When you cook, you get everything out—
not a recollective gene in your body, yet
I am homebound, house-drunk on you,

intolerant as the moon of another orbit—
sole, lonely planet to follow yours,
through this universe and beyond,
heaven or hell, fire or ice.

Where we end,
we end together.
Beyond this,
I need know nothing else.

Questions

What is the prerogative of the dying?
Denial, reticence,
anger,
grace?

What presents do we bear the swaddled one?
Melancholy, laughter,
reminisces,
tears?

A day remains—
perhaps an hour,
or moments to settle
what has taken much time.

Do we close doors
or leave them ajar?
Do we cower from the coming storm
or stand blithely in its path?

In memoriam—Meredith Lund 1947–2015

Uses of Lie and Lay and the 5:30 AM
Friday Morning Incident

The heifer was lying with a broken back when we found her.
We shot and dragged her off the road and laid her in the pasture.

The driver was lying, said *thirty* was all he'd been doing.
I left for hospice to Mother's bedside, where she lay dying.

Daybreak revealed another heifer lying near the first,
and another lay in the ditch, thrown there by force.

Despite a suspended license, the driver laid claim to innocence,
as lying scattered on the road, his car in parts and pieces.

The butcher laid the heifers on his trailer with a hoist.
The adjuster said, *"Blame lies on an open gate and whoever let*

them out—lay it on a wicked or a hapless soul at best."
Several days later, we laid Mother to rest.

The Way

Give yourself to mouths that eat,
the slash of claws and grasp of teeth.
Let every harm come to pass, sleep
beneath treading feet.

May all voices speak your name,
and other pockets hold your loss
as all your riches turn to dross,
and wither in consuming flame.

Keep your silence and forget,
gladly forfeit and accept
your whole demise with hope and love,
You are the Earth's and its fullness thereof.

The Ugly Bull

We had to castrate a large black Brahman-cross bull calf born out of season—he was the epitome of ugliness, too much ear, overgrown, wild, wrong in time and place, the result of an unplanned liaison between his Brahman mother and a cull bull that broke through the fence. We saved the task for the afternoon out of dread, and there was discussion at lunch where he belonged, and what to do. On our return we determined to cut him. *He's only worth what he's worth, balls or no,* I started to reason with Boss, but there was a challenge in the air out of the simple, farm-made fact it should be done—if he was headed to the butcher, we'd send him in a proper state.

You'll have to do him standing up he said, looking at me *You know how?* I said *Tell me* hoping to hear something new. *Pole him up close, get in behind, make your cut, pull each testicle out and cut it with the emasculators as if we had him on the ground.* We ran him in the chute and scotched him tight. He tried to wrench free. I took a bucket of disinfectant and tools through the palpation gate, kneeled, reaching for the scrotum, handled it a moment for a reaction. The bull shifted weight. I held the bucket close and doused the scrotum with handfuls of the cold solution, thinking this would earn me a good kicking. The bull stood still.

Bonnie's Poem

No one has ever written
a poem for me, She said,
not one word for all my
meanderings outside
the country of love.

—

Tonight I hug my pillow.
It's never early or late
to know love.
Exile from my heart—
your love dwells in me,

ever returning,
and mine for you—
ever departing.
Love keeps in each of us
a place named *Forever*.

translated for Hildegarde Sexton by her son

The Last Load

In memoriam—Otis Baldwin 1954–2011

Alton stands by the gate at dusk,
the last load of bees on the truck, and Otis
is on the forklift pulling the little trailer free
from a soft place in the pasture.

We're headed to Alabama, this is our last load
Alton says; mosquitoes fierce as we stand
talking and swatting the biting air.
He says, *You really got 'em down here!*

I don't know why I'm this old and still foolin' with bees—
I guess I just love it. Otis and I have about 700 colonies.
We want to get them up to around two thousand.
You'll see a few boxes out there when we're gone,
left for the stragglers. They'll be safe here
until we come back for 'em later.
Hauling 'em at night, we'll be sure
to get most, but some are still out there—
A bee'll go over two miles after pollen and nectar.
If it gets dark, he'll spend the night out,
come home in the mornin' light.

———

Otis became Charley Jewett's partner when he moved to Graceville.
They put bees on the ranch three years, hauling truckloads
from north Florida, but Charley quit coming without a word,
He done fell out with his wife—Otis said,
She changed the lock on the do', up and sold his cows on him.
He been stayin' in a shed, keepin' bees somewhere
I don't know, ever since. He done gone his way, I gone
mine. I got up with Alton—been with him a year
We figured we'd come and find some places down
here and you might let us locate for the pepper-tree bloom.

I showed them the South ditchbank line just before noon
and told them, *Gruwell's on the new land, Charles Smith's*
to the North—you can go here without bothering anyone.
When will you come? Otis said *Rule of thumb is*
set up by Labor Day to catch the pepper bloom.
Will you leave the honey on through winter or take some off?
Might get a couple hunderd boxes—if they's enough.
Is it best to take it all and sugar 'em when it gets cold?
No, we like 'em to carry they own groceries through the do'.
We'll let them keep all they want—if it's been a good bloom.

———

A semi-trailer arrived, stacked its length with hives—
covered with black screen cloth and barely passed
through the gate on the road to park on the first bed.
It soon filled with multi-colored boxes, four to the palette,
as if a rainbow had broken over the field into large pieces.

Alton said *Now don't think nothin' of all the different colors,*
We buy paint when it's cheap and we aren't particular.
They worked all morning, and it rained the whole while.
With the trailer finally empty, the driver left for Graceville
as they started taking bees out to where they'd spend the winter.

How about bad weather, does it keep them in?
Oh honey bees will go out in the rain,
They're the hardest workingest little creatures on earth.
We can tend 'em when its wet—certainly,
but do so only if we're in a hurry.

I called Alton at six, as I was locking the bridge gate.
They were shopping motel rooms out by the interstate.
I made a few suggestions and said, *I thought you'd be
puttin' out hives half the night.*
Oh we can work 'em in the dark, but we prefer daylight.

You see—that's when they fly, and you control them with smoke.
They'll sting anytime, but they crawl after dark
and you never know where they're going.
You'll get 'em up your sleeve, or pants leg and under your veil,
so we always prefer to work 'em when they're flying."

———

My bee-education continued one afternoon, under the barn
during a downpour. Otis and Alton had backed their truck in
and were loading extra *supers* they'd stored for the next bloom
beneath the stairs. A few escaped bees were buzzing around us
as we stood waiting. Alton said *What goes on in the hive is
determined by* them, *they're all females. The queen can't even
feed herself. She's taken care of by drones—the only males in
the whole hive. Fortunate for us, a honeybee doesn't know to
quit. Long as there's nectar, she'll keep bringing it in. When
the hive is full, she'll make burr-comb, even fill spaces outside
between the boxes, and make more honey. She won't stop, long
as she's alive.*

As he spoke, I watched Otis deftly tying empty boxes down—
cinching the rope in grabs, pulling and holding, pulling again,
pinching slack secure in a half-hitch looped on itself for quick
release, feeding the latch-end through, wrapping extra around
tight. He tied each row alike—cinching and fastening without
a word 'til he was done.

———

104

One morning in early winter, I answered the phone: *This is Alton—I 'm calling with bad news:*
Yesterday Otis died in his sleep.
His wife said he'd felt bad for several days;
he went straight to bed after work and never woke up.

He was on heart medication, but we thought it was under control.
We had to stop and let him rest, moving bees a week ago.
Usually, when we worked, he never quit all day.
I thought nothing of it. When we got back home
he went straight to the doctor's, but they figured he was OK.

I don't know what I'm going to do without him; his service is in a day or two. We've been over to see his wife several times—
I want you to know I don't have it all figured out, but things aren't going to change—I'll be there next year one way or another. I hope his son will want to keep the business.
We'll come for orange blossom next Spring. I aim to never stop takin' care of bees.

Anniversary

No matter we drew the curtains—
the waking breeze opens
and folds them like the sea,

and though we welcomed the dark—
morning bids its departure
through every window, every door.

We were but children when we met—
now silver gathers in your hair like a dusting
of snow on the mountains in June.

List of Images

Notes

"The Prosperous Year" pg. 4

Drawn largely upon the 2014 spring and summer when we saw and received unprecedented prices for all ages and classes of cattle due to supply side factors in the industry. *All's I can say is get it while you can,* came from a roadside conversation with my cow neighbor, Mr. Charlie Hamner, and the saying, *The cure for high prices is high prices,* was stated to me by three different cattlemen at a bar in the Marco Island Marriott Resort following the sale: Jim Strickland, Woody Larson, and Jim Farley. Farley also said, *Boys take heed—this is a boom, it ain't going to last forever! I set two personal records this morning at the Producer's sale: I sold a load of calves for more money than I ever got before, and I paid more money for a load of calves than I ever have my whole life!*

"How Vultures Eat a Cow" pg. 6

As told by Bob Montanaro, and from lifelong observation.

"Physiology of Bovine Reproduction" pg. 12

This was written in a motel room in Okeechobee just prior to the morning Fall Quarterly Board of Director's Meeting of the Florida Cattlemen's Association. Much of the information was gleaned from a *Reproductive Physiology of Farm Animals* text and "Anatomy and Physiology of Bovine Reproduction" course taught by Dr. Alvin Warnick and Dr. Michael Fields at the University of Florida, conversations with Maarten Drost, DVM, Jim Harvey, DVM, and Dr. Joel Yelich, as well as a lifetime of observation and practice of bovine obstetrics and breeding throughout decades of calving seasons on Treasure Hammock Ranch.

"Calving Season in the Tropics" pg. 13

Fall calving in most of Florida is the custom; however, the November start of the season, resulting from a late December to early February beginning of the breeding season was originally determined to bring calves after the end of hurricane Season for obvious reasons. Nonetheless, calves (and everything else) are subject to the tumult of late storms accompanying summer's end.

"Planting Aeschynomene Seed" pg. 20

Aeschynoneme is a warm-season annual legume adapted to moist sites throughout the state but is mainly grown in south Florida. It is high in protein and nutrients, and is palatable to cattle and customarily "inoculated" with bacteria specific to the *Cowpea group* to infect the roots enabling the plant and soil to benefit from its nitrogen-fixing properties. The process of inoculating legume seed outlined in the poem, including the use of buttermilk as a "sticker," has been handed down from father to son for four generations on Treasure Hammock Ranch.

"Elko" pg. 28

Elko, Nevada: home of the Western Folklife Center and setting of the weeklong National Cowboy Poetry Gathering which takes place in early winter each year. In 2017 the Gathering celebrated its 34th Anniversary with performance, poetry, music, humor, arts and craft presentations, and subjects of special interest to ecology and culture of the West.

"Disparate" pg. 32

Giorgio Morandi [1890–1964] was an Italian modernist painter and printmaker who specialized in still life and landscape subjects in his native Bologna where he lived with his three sisters, Ana, Dina, and Maria Teresa until his death.

Roberto Longhi was an Italian academic, critic, and close friend of Morandi.

"Above Portland" pg. 34

Childe Hassam [1859–1935] was a nineteenth-century American impressionist painter noted for urban and coastal scenes. In 1904 and 1908 he traveled to Oregon, painted out of doors with his friend, Col. C.E. Woodhouse producing over 100 paintings, pastels, and watercolors including images of Mt. Hood from elevations in an area now known as Washington Park overlooking the Willamette River Valley.

Notes

"Cow Landays" pg. 64

Most likely brought by Aryan caravans thousands of years ago, these folk couplets are traditionally sung. Often anonymous, they were created by and for mostly illiterate people: the more than twenty million Pashtun women living in the region between Afghanistan and Pakistan.

Landays present five main subjects: war, separation, grief, love, and land. They are often sung aloud to the beat of a hand drum. Each poem has twenty-two syllables, nine in the first line, thirteen in the second, sometimes rhyming but more often not, and lilt internally from word to word in a kind of lullaby that belies the acuity of their content.

An excellent introduction to Landays can be found in *Poetry* [June 2013] by Eliza Griswold.

The epigraph by Aeschylus is borrowed (with humility) from Seamus Heaney's book, *Death of the Naturalist* in his absence.

"Stay" pg. 87

This poem was written on the front porch of the Laura (Riding) Jackson house, now preserved and maintained by a local literary foundation in her name. Laura and Schuyler Jackson moved to the original homestead in Wabasso, FL, in 1943 to grow and pack citrus, as well as rewrite (and re-order) the English dictionary on the premise that every word has a precise use and meaning. They were hard-working, exacting figures of far-flung notoriety, with voluminous correspondences, and colorful pasts, living in Florida's often harsh ambient conditions with well-water and kerosene light. Pre-deceased by Schuyler, Laura saw their seminal *A Case for Rational Meaning* to completion, published after she died in 1991 at the age of 91.

"Three Dried Lemons" pg. 91

In the etching process, it is possible to create variable gradations in tone by *staging* the duration of the etch of the plate, stopping out the action of the acid with *asphaltum* or commercial *stop-out varnish* in some areas as other areas remain untreated and continue to etch. The longer the etch, the deeper the lines and darker the registration of the image. Prints from etched plates always present a mirror image of the original subject, accounting for the reversed appearance of script and numbers etched in the plate.

"The Last Load" pg. 102

There are several economically significant periods of nectar production from blooms (also called *flows*) of indigenous as well as *introduced* plants in Southeast coastal Florida throughout the year attracting apiaries around the country to travel to and locate bees on agricultural lands in the region, taking advantage of resulting honey crops. These include Palmetto, Brazilian Pepper, Orange Blossom, Gallberry and, in more northerly marshland locations, Tupelo. There are also ongoing, less significant and mostly wild flower sources of nectar including Spanish needle, native clovers, and legumes, cabbage palm, and a whole plethora of plant varieties producing nectar year-round. *Supers* are the larger additional boxes stacked on top of beehives that contain frames of foundation and comb for the bees to fill with honey during a flow. These are separated from the bottom hive by excluder screens designed to keep the queen below, where she goes about her business laying eggs in the brood chamber.

Sean Sexton was born in Indian River County and grew up on his family's Treasure Hammock Ranch. He divides his time between taking care of a 600-acre cow-calf operation, painting, sculpting, and writing. He is married to artist Sharon Sexton, and they live on the ranch in a house they built with their hands. He has kept daily sketch and written journals since 1973. He received an Individual Artist's Fellowship from the State of Florida in 2000. He is author of *Waldo's Mountain*, 2004, Waterview Press, *Blood Writing, Poems*, Anhinga Press, 2009, *The Empty Tomb*, University of Alabama Slash Pine Press, 2014 and *Descent*, Yellow Jacket Press, 2017.

He has presented regularly since 2009 at the National Cowboy Poetry Gathering in Elko, Nevada, and became the inaugural Poet Laureate of Indian River County by resolution on Sept 1, 2016.

Coda

Light is an airless wind
sending otherness to shadow,
it does not give, it only lends
what matter merely borrows

www.ingramcontent.com/pod-product-compliance
Lightning Source LLC
Chambersburg PA
CBHW021405090426
42742CB00009B/1018